#elpful ashtags

Conversation Starters, Wisdom Nuggets and Devotionals to Help With Decision Making

FRANCHETTA DUDLEY

FOREWORD BY DR. TRAVIS C. JENNINGS

Editing: Franchetta Dudley

Printed in the United States of America
Keen Vision Publishing, LLC
www.keen-vision.com
ISBN: 978-1-948270-49-6

To everyone in pursuit of their dreams and purpose. May this book empower and encourage you to become the best version of you, push past your fears, and positively impact the lives of others.

Franchetta Dudley

Contents

FOREWORD

The "ability to dream again after experiencing a nightmare," is the title of one of the most impactful messages I've preached, so I am told. Although it was years ago, this message still resounds with people even years later. How exactly do you dream again if you've experienced nightmare after nightmare? Better yet, how can you effectively navigate life once the nightmare is over? More often, nightmares are worries, fears or life-anomalies that manifest within our subconscious mind. It's our mind's mechanism of coping with what worries us, what's causing anxiety or its way of warning us of some impending danger. However, real problems arise when these fears, worries or anomalies aren't addressed effectively and timely or when the nightmares actually exit the subconscious and become our reality.

There must be intentionality when learning "how to dream again." In essence, how do you train your mind – your subconscious to hope again? To believe again? How do you counteract current but false reality with a new reality and equipment for navigating life? How do you ensure that the decisions you make this time won't lead to more nightmares? Enter: *Helpful Hashtags: Conversation Starters, Wisdom Nuggets, and Devotionals to Help with Decision Making!*

Franchetta Dudley has beautifully crafted a catalogue of practical thoughts to assist in not only helping dreamers dream again, but she provides a step-by-step guide to effectively navigate life or a new reality. A dreamer herself, Franchetta can tell you all about nightmares, but what I enjoy about her approach is that she has paid very close attention to the lessons she's learned during those nightmare seasons. She has applied those lessons learned to her personal life, and she has compiled an arsenal of wisdom; locked and fully-loaded for the next season of her life.

Franchetta is passionate as much as she is intentional about helping people successfully navigate through the nightmares of life and even life after the nightmares, just as she has found the courage to. She's a conqueror and wants other conquerors to grow in wisdom and strength as you'll discover while reading her life-application manual. In *Helpful Hashtags*, she offers readers the equipment and life resources that can be practically applied right now. In this prophecy-driven time, I'm glad to know there are emerging voices who are not only concerned about where you're going, but they are just as concerned about how you get there.

As an Apostle, I've had the honor of cultivating the growth and matriculation of several authors under my tutelage, and I'm very proud to have participated in the launch of Franchetta Dudley's project.

Helpful Hashtags: Conversation Starters, Wisdom Nuggets and Devotionals To Help with Decision Making is not just another book, but it is a practical resource that you'll want to reference over and over and from cover to cover...again and again.

Dr. Travis C. Jennings
Life Coach and Author of the following published works:
The Gathering of Champions: It's Time to Get in the Ring
Life on Turbo
Lifeguard: Help is on the Way
Faith for the Gold

INTRODUCTION

First and foremost, thank you for purchasing *Helpful Hashtags*. It is an honor to know that you are reading my book and that you have the opportunity to learn and be encouraged from my journey. This book was inspired by an idea I had to decorate my classroom wall with principles and wisdom for life and success coined with a hashtag. While working on and sitting with this idea, I attended a special Prophetic Encounter church service at Harvest Tabernacle Church in Lithonia, Georgia where Apostle Travis Jennings prayed for me. When I arrived home from the service, God spoke to me and said, "*Helpful Hashtags* is not just for your classroom; it's a book." He then gave me the subtitle, "*Conversation Starters, Wisdom Nuggets, and Devotionals to Help with Decision Making.*"

Throughout my life, as long as I can remember, I have always been that person with whom people felt comfortable with bearing their soul to, confiding in, or practically sharing their whole life story. For some reason, they felt like what I said would make a difference. As I would listen to these various people, sometimes friends, family, and complete strangers, I would give them advice and guidance practically and prayerfully to the best of my ability. Oftentimes, this was difficult for me to accept because I felt inadequate or unworthy despite the many testimonies people would bring back to me as a result of my advice and counsel. I would often ask myself and God, "Why does this keep happening to me?" One day, the light came on, and I realized that it was a grace and gift given to me from God, to whom I will be eternally thankful.

As I wrote, I realized that each hashtag represented wisdom, truths, and realities I had to learn on my journey of experiencing growth, change, transitions, and victories as well as overcoming disappointments, challenges and hurt. There was a lesson for me in every experience that made me a better person. And what good is a testimony or a lesson if you don't share it?

As you read *Helpful Hashtags*, purpose to apply them to your life and use them as tools to help others in their decision making processes. With each personal application take time to journal and write down your reflections. Introspective reflections are often the beginning of making healthier decisions. We cannot address in others what we don't have the courage to address in ourselves. On the other side of honesty with ourselves and God is a priceless freedom and healing that is worth the process. I thank God for giving me the inspiration to share my insights and lessons with you through *Helpful Hashtags*. With some of the hashtags, scriptures are recorded for you. And with others, just the scripture reference is given for you to look up on your own and keep you interactive. My prayer is that *Helpful Hashtags* is an interactive read that will add more lessons and testimonies to your life that will bless you and others.

TRUST THE PROCESS
Devotional

#TRUSTTHEPROCESS

"And let us not grow weary while doing good, for in due season we shall reap if we do not lose heart."

Galatians 6:9 (NKJV)

If you believe God has designed a purpose and destiny for your life, you must accept, trust, and submit to the process necessary to get you there. A process is a series of actions or steps taken to achieve a particular end. Processes are usually uncomfortable methods of doing or making something into a finished product. The most significant benefit of enduring any life process is uncovering our purpose. Since we all have unique purposes, we must be careful not to compare our process to others. Our process will teach us five things:

1. How to be patient in suffering.
2. How to embrace delayed gratification.
3. How to allow God to avenge us.
4. How to understand God's timing.
5. How to handle promotion.

Where are you in your process to purpose? Are you embracing it or neglecting it?

Thoughts and Reflections

_____

_____

_____

_____

_____

_____

#TRUSTTHEPROCESS

LOSING TO WIN

Wisdom Nugget

#SOMETIMESYOUHAVETOLOSETOWIN

I f all we do is win, we would never learn how to handle and overcome loss. The failures we experience in life help us create strategies to win. All is not lost in loss. There is always a lesson gained to position us for a win next time. What are some of the lessons you have learned in a loss? Did you apply these lessons? Did you share them with someone who can benefit from what you learned? If not, it's time to do so. Remember, lessons learned in failures can help you and others. The blessing is in the lesson.

Thoughts and Reflections

_____

_____

_____

_____

_____

_____

_____

_____

_____

_____

_____

_____

_____

_____

_____

DIVINE CONNECTIONS

Wisdom Nugget

#DIVINECONNECTIONS

It is human nature to desire to connect with people. In His divine nature, God connects us with other people. If we live our lives only connecting with those we want to connect with, we will miss the opportunity to develop invaluable relationships. We should live our lives open and receptive to God's divinely planned connections. Take a moment right now and declare that God is giving you divine connections. If you are open, God can give you connections that:

- Don't have any hidden agendas or ulterior motives.
- Serve a purpose in your purpose.
- Make you a better person and steward over your life.
- Come with mutual benefits.

Wouldn't you like these types of connections? They are waiting for you. Believe it, expect it, and receive it.

Thoughts and Reflections

ENCOURAGE SOMEONE

Wisdom Nugget

#ENCOURAGESOMEONETODAY

Encouragement will never go out of style. Every day, we come in contact with individuals who need encouragement. No man or woman is an island. We all experience difficult times that test our faith and the core of who we are. Though often unsaid, even the encourager needs encouragement. How does it make you feel when someone genuinely encourages you? I imagine that it feels great, life-changing, and honorable, right? Why not pass these same feelings on to others? Have you encouraged someone this week? How can you encourage someone today?

Thoughts and Reflections

_____

_____

_____

_____

_____

_____

_____

_____

_____

_____

_____

_____

_____

_____

_____

DON'T TAKE IT PERSONAL

Conversation Starter

#DONTTAKEITPERSONALPERMANENTLY

"But if you have bitter envy and self-seeking in your hearts, do not boast and lie against the truth. This wisdom does not descend from above, but is earthly, sensual, demonic. For where envy and self-seeking exist, confusion and every evil thing are there."

James 3:14-16 (NKJV)

D on't take it personal," is often said and advised before or after an offense. However, the root word of personal is "person." There is no way to separate the two. The truth is, we don't always automatically resolve not to take something personal. At times, offensive actions and statements take time to process and get over. Some people take longer than others to process. Getting over an offense is often a self-journeyed process that can't always be dictated or demanded by the offender. The ultimate goal is not to take it personal permanently. More importantly, don't let it make you bitter. Let it make you better. Are you holding on to any offenses that you need to process and forgive others for?

Thoughts and Reflections

FIGHT FOR IT
Devotional

#FIGHTFORIT

"And from the days of John the Baptist until now the kingdom of heaven suffers violence, and the violent take it by force."

Matthew 11:12 (NKJV)

The promises you are believing God for won't always come easily. II Corinthians 10:3-5 (NIV) gives us this counsel, "For though we live in the world, we do not wage war as the world does. The weapons we fight with are not the weapons of the world. On the contrary, they have divine power to demolish strongholds. We demolish arguments and every pretension that sets itself up against the knowledge of God, and we take captive every thought to make it obedient to Christ." We fight in the spirit with the word of God, prayer, praise, worship and fasting. Are you using your spiritual weapons? Sometimes, you must fight for His promises in the spirit. Don't be afraid to fight for whatever you are believing God for concerning your purpose, healing, deliverance, family, and finances. Don't allow the enemy to have a field day with your mind and steal what rightfully belongs to you and your family. Keep your fight alive!

Thoughts and Reflections

_____

_____

_____

_____

_____

_____

_____

_____

USE YOUR VOICE

Conversation Starter

#USEYOURVOICE

Know your voice, define your voice, and never lose your voice. God gave you a voice to be heard, to reinforce your self-worth, and to add value to the lives of others – all for His glory. What should you be saying, promoting, advocating, or writing? Think about it. How can you get started? When will you get started? If we don't use our voice, we often lose our voice and allow others to assume our voice. Today, how can you begin making your voice count and creating a platform for your voice to be heard?

Thoughts and Reflections

_____

_____

_____

_____

_____

_____

_____

_____

_____

_____

_____

_____

_____

_____

DON'T BOX GOD IN

Devotional

#DONTBOXGODIN

"For my thoughts are not your thoughts, neither are your ways my ways," declares the LORD. As the heavens are higher than the earth, so are my ways higher than your ways and my thoughts than your thoughts."

Isaiah 55:8-9 (NIV)

God can do what He wants and how He wants to do it at any time. He can move in any way He wants to through whoever He wants to at any given time or place. God has over one thousand different ways He can bless you. Let that sink in for a moment. We often box God in because we look for Him to move the way we were taught or in ways that we have seen Him move before. God may not do it for you, the way He did it for your mother, father, grandmother, or friend. Don't limit your thinking to this level but rather think outside of the box. God has some authentic, fresh encounters and blessings for you that can't be perceived or received with a one-dimensional or biased mindset. Are there some things in your life right now that you have limited yourself in because you can only see it happening one way or only through certain persons? Have you become discouraged because of an unanswered prayer? God could very well be teaching you not to limit Him to moving one way. Changing your thinking, can change your receiving.

Thoughts and Reflections

_____

_____

_____

_____

_____

_____

#DONTBOXGODIN

BE INTENTIONAL

Conversation Starter

#BEINTENTIONAL

To get something you have never received before, you must do something you have never done before. This is a time and era where we must be intentional. To be intentional simply means to be purpose driven. Don't allow your words, actions, conversations, connections, praise, or worship to God to be casual. Do everything with intentionality. You will have what you say, reap what you sow, and accomplish what you target. How intentional are you being about life and accomplishing your goals? Embracing intentionality will yield more desired results.

Thoughts and Reflections

_____

_____

_____

_____

_____

_____

_____

_____

_____

_____

_____

_____

_____

_____

MATTERS OF THE HEART
Devotional

"But the things that come out of person's mouth come from the heart, and these defile them."

Matthew 15:18 (NIV)

Getting to know the heart of a person is not something that happens quick. It takes time to know a person's heart towards you and God. When you have concerns or doubt about where a person's heart is, don't try to figure it out on your own. Ask God to show you the heart of a person before you open or give your heart away. God will often show us a person's heart by the words they say. What comes out of a person's mouth is a strong indication of how they feel in their heart. In relationships, these principles go both ways. The same way we assess the words of others we must assess our words. Also, we can't honestly get to know the heart of a person when our hearts are not right towards God and we are void of self-love. "And you shall love the Lord your God with all your heart and with all your soul and with all your strength. This is the first commandment. And the second is this: 'Love your neighbor as yourself. There is no other commandment greater than these," (Mark 12:30-31, NKJV). Do your words reflect what's in your heart? How well are you managing the issues of your heart with others?

Thoughts and Reflections

_____

_____

_____

_____

_____

RELATIONSHIPS 101

Wisdom Nugget

#RELATIONSHIPS101

In order to have healthy relationships, there must be reciprocity. Reciprocity is the process of exchanging things with others for mutual benefit. There should be no one-sided relationships. At times, relationships go through periods when one person is stronger or more successful than the other. During these times, making adjustments to maintain the relationship is necessary, but not a license to be used. In every relationship, there should be shared benefits. Know the difference between a supporter and a leech. Are there relationships in your life to which you need to make adjustments? Is it time for a conversation about reciprocity?

Thoughts and Reflections

_____

_____

_____

_____

_____

_____

_____

_____

_____

_____

_____

_____

DON'T SETTLE
Conversation Starter

#DONTSETTLEFORAVERAGE

Where there is no hope, there is no expectation. Without expectation, one is bound to go through life settling for average. Average represents that which is ordinary and mediocre. Why settle for being average when you have every thing within you to be extraordinary and creative? Yes, you! Is there anything in your life keeping you from becoming the best you can be? Are you maximizing the gifts and talents you possess? Declare today, "I have hope. I believe in myself and expect nothing less than the best for me. I will never settle for being average."

Thoughts and Reflections

_____

_____

_____

_____

_____

_____

_____

_____

_____

_____

_____

_____

_____

_____

_____

_____

KEEP YOUR WORD
Devotional

#KEEPINGYOURWORDMATTERS

"It is better not to make a vow than to make one and not fulfill it."

Ecclesiastes 5:5 (NIV)

Keeping one's word is a valuable asset in life. Saying one thing and doing another can lead to a loss of respect and a lack of trust from others. Don't say it if you don't mean it. Don't commit to it if you cannot do it. Be careful not to make rash vows to God or others out of fear, guilt, shame and pressure or without proper research and investigation. Is there anyone you need to make your word good to? Is there something you told God you would do but have not done it yet?

Thoughts and Reflections

_____

_____

_____

_____

_____

_____

_____

_____

_____

_____

_____

_____

_____

_____

_____

#KEEPINGYOURWORDMATTERS

BE ACCOUNTABLE

Conversation Starter

#BEACCOUNTABLE

Who's holding you accountable? Everyone needs good accountability. If everybody who sits on the front seat of your life does not challenge you to grow and help you become a better person, there is an accountability failure. We all need someone to help us clear up the blind spots caused by our self-imposed biases. Are the right people sitting on the front seat of your life? Accountability partners should be stronger than you in the areas they are holding you accountable. Moreover, those that hold you accountable should be people that can give you a safe place to hurt and heal and check you when you're wrong. Also, accountability partners support you by giving constructive criticism and positive reinforcement as you implement the counsel they provide. Accountability requires a balance of instruction, correction, love and grace.

Thoughts and Reflections

_____

_____

_____

_____

_____

_____

_____

_____

_____

_____

SECOND WIND

Wisdom Nugget

#THEPOWEROFASECONDWIND

Athletes often speak of the power of getting a second wind when they feel like giving up. A second wind is a new strength to continue or to start over after feeling unable to go on. You may feel like quitting or giving up, but you can't. Why? You are too close to the finish line. God will give you a second wind to finish what you started. Declare today, "Lord, thank you for giving me a second wind to pursue my goals, visions, and dreams. I will finish strong." Again, you are too close to the finish line. No matter how tired, behind or inadequate you may feel, giving up is not an option. You are in position to regain your strength and endurance.

Thoughts and Reflections

_____

_____

_____

_____

_____

_____

_____

_____

_____

_____

_____

_____

_____

_____

RESPECT 101
Wisdom Nugget

#RESPECT101

Once respect is lost for someone, it rarely returns to its original height. Respect is most often lost through the repeated failure to keep one's word and when one's actions repeatedly don't match their words. Let's strive each day to maintain our respect levels with conviction and integrity. One should not be expected to respect that which they have not experienced in words and deeds. More importantly, one should never demand respect without first having given respect. What are your thoughts on giving and receiving respect? Are you giving as much respect to people as you expect them to give to you? In some of your relationships, does the respect you give need to level up?

Thoughts and Reflections

_____

_____

_____

_____

_____

_____

_____

_____

_____

_____

_____

_____

PEOPLE VS GOD

Devotional

#PEOPLEVSGOD

"The LORD is my light and my salvation so why should I be afraid? The LORD is my fortress, protecting me from danger, so why should I tremble? When evil people come to devour me, when my enemies and foes attack me, they will stumble and fall."

Psalm 27:1-2 (NLT)

In this day and age, everyone is a critic. Sometimes, the wrong people will have opinions about who we are and what we do. While God allows us to be delivered from many things, the most powerful freedom we will ever experience is freedom from the thoughts and opinions of the wrong people. Who's putting their undesired opinions all over your purpose? Have you given them clearance to speak into your life? What does their life say about their ability to produce? I don't know about you, but today seems like the perfect day to free yourself from the opinions and word curses of people. People's opinions will never have power over God's words. Take time to think about this question: Is there anyone in your life that you are allowing to define you above God?

Thoughts and Reflections

_____

_____

_____

_____

_____

_____

_____

_____

_____

EMOTIONS
Conversation Starter

#DONTLETYOUREMOTIONSCLOUDTRUTH

When making tough decisions, identifying and accepting the facts in situations will help neutralize and eliminate our emotions. Facts don't lie, however, our emotions tend to cloud truth. Nothing can be more regretful than looking back on a situation where you allowed your emotions to lead you down the wrong path. Be careful not to dismiss facts because you are too afraid or self-centered to accept the truth. How well are you managing your emotions in life? How well do you accept difficult truths? How can you improve your ability to control your emotions?

Thoughts and Reflections

_____

_____

_____

_____

_____

_____

_____

_____

_____

_____

_____

_____

_____

_____

CAPTURE INSPIRATION

Conversation Starter

#CAPTUREINSPIRATIONFROMGOD

Motivation is given intentionally by others and must be nurtured outwardly. Inspiration is received spontaneously from others and must be nurtured inwardly. Inspiration from others is good, but inspiration from God is priceless. One of the most powerful things to receive from God is inspiration. Inspiration, when captured, has the potential to take us from poverty to prosperity and from obscurity to notoriety. How are you capturing your inspirational moments in life and with God? Do you keep pen and paper nearby or have a recording device ready? Once you capture this inspiration, activate, develop and package it into something tangible. What are some things you can start doing to ensure that you create the space and time to capture these moments?

Thoughts and Reflections

_____

_____

_____

_____

_____

_____

_____

_____

_____

_____

_____

_____

HEART CHECK

Devotional

#CHECKYOURHEART

"The human heart is the most deceitful of all things, and desperately wicked. Who really knows how bad it is? But I, the Lord, search all hearts and examine secret motives."

Jeremiah 17:9-10 (NLT)

Many of us have advised others with the phrase, "Follow your heart." However, the heart can be deceiving if it is not rooted in the word of God and spiritual discernment. Something can be in our heart but not in God's will. Ask God to uncover what's in your heart and provide you with insight to His heart and will concerning your life. King David prayed a very simple but profound prayer that we can pray daily to check our hearts. "Let the words of my mouth and the meditations of my heart be acceptable in Your sight oh Lord my strength and my redeemer," (Psalm 19:14 NKJV). Are you committed to doing a heart check daily?

Thoughts and Reflections

_____

_____

_____

_____

_____

_____

_____

_____

_____

_____

GUARD YOUR EYE GATES

Devotional

#GUARDYOUREYEGATES

"Your eye is like a lamp that provides light for your body. When your eye is healthy, your whole body is filled with light. But when your eye is unhealthy, your whole body is filled with darkness. And if the light you have is actually darkness, how deep that darkness is!"

Matthew 6:22-23 (NLT)

Our eyes are two of the most sensitive and influential parts of our body. The eyes are often referred to as windows to the soul. I describe them as doorways to the mind. It is vital for us to guard our eye gates. We must become our eyes' personal security guards to ensure that everything we see has been carefully identified as acceptable and beneficial, not counterproductive to achieving our goals and maintaining good character. In light of the extremely liberal and elicit climate in the media, protecting our eyes from negative stimuli requires intentionality. If not, our eyesight will become immune and desensitized to the effects of the media. What looks good to our eyes is not always good for our system. Unhealthy visualization can lead to internal contamination. The eyes should be channels of good and light, not evil and darkness.

Thoughts and Reflections

_____

_____

_____

_____

_____

_____

#GUARDYOUREYEGATES

THE WORD OF GOD
Devotional

Our relationship with God is more important than any relationship we will ever have. Our relationship with Him can be no stronger than our relationship with His word. The Word of God is a lamp unto our feet, and a light unto our pathway and the entrance into God's Word gives light (Psalm 119:105, 130). The Word of God discerns and exposes our most inner thoughts and desires (Hebrews 4:12). It corrects us when we are wrong and teaches us to do what is right (II Timothy 3:16). Nurture, establish and build your relationship with the Word of God. One word from God can change and save your life. How consistent are you in reading and getting an understanding of the word of God? What's the last insight or revelation you received from the word of God to apply to your life?

Thoughts and Reflections

_____

_____

_____

_____

_____

_____

_____

_____

_____

_____

_____

_____

#HAVEARELATIONSHIPWITHTHEWORDOFGOD

MAKE PRAYER A LIFESTYLE

Devotional

#MAKEPRAYERALIFESTYLE

"Now He was telling them a parable to show that at all times they ought to pray and not to lose heart."

Luke 18:1 (NASB)

Believing in the power of prayer is one of the best decisions we can make in our lives. Prayer is how we communicate with God. Through prayer, we learn to hear His voice. We must discipline ourselves to talk to God about our lives, struggles, feelings, purposes, dreams, relationships, desires, needs, and wants. A healthy prayer life will keep us in perfect peace in even the most difficult situations. Unlike our conversations with people, God can always be trusted with our deepest pains and smallest concerns. We must be careful not to spend more time talking to people than God. God should not be an afterthought that we run to after we make a mess of things. We should get in the habit of seeking God before we make plans in our lives. To help build a consistent prayer life, create a space daily where you can pray to God. Have you prayed today? On a scale from 1-10, how would you rate your prayer life? What are some realistic and tangible ways you can improve your prayer life?

Thoughts and Reflections

_____

_____

_____

_____

_____

_____

_____

#MAKEPRAYERALIFESTYLE

DON'T ASSUME

Wisdom Nugget

It's normal to want to help our family and friends when we see them going in the wrong direction, needing help in an area or repeating the same mistakes over and over again. However, we must remember that everybody does not want our help or advice. Consequently, at times when our help or advice is not accepted or appreciated, we tend to get upset or feel offended. Ironically, God often during these times wants them to learn a lesson only He can teach them. The question you must ask yourself is, did they invite you in or did you invite yourself into their situation. Help or advice is often best received by invitation rather than unsolicited obligation. What's your take or approach on giving advice? How do you feel when your advice is not taken or criticized? You have valuable knowledge and experience to help others, but remember you can't force it in, it is best to be invited in.

Thoughts and Reflections

_____

_____

_____

_____

_____

_____

_____

_____

_____

SPEAK LIFE
Devotional

#SPEAKLIFEINTOYOURSITUATION

"For verily I say unto you, That whosoever shall say unto this mountain, be thou removed, and be thou cast into the sea; and shall not doubt in his heart, but shall believe that those things which he saith shall come to pass; he shall have whatsoever he saith."

Mark 11:23 (KJV)

Words have creative power. Death and life are in the power of the tongue (Proverbs 18:21). Whatever we magnify with our mouths will be magnified in our lives. Call those things that are not, as though they were, for we will have what we say. What do you see in your life? Is it possible that you are in your current predicament because you spoke it into existence? Take a moment to make some positive confessions and declarations over your day and destiny. Take it a step further and write them down to confess and declare daily starting today.

Thoughts and Reflections

_____

_____

_____

_____

_____

_____

_____

_____

_____

_____

_____

#SPEAKLIFEINTOYOURSITUATION

OWN YOUR PROCESS

Conversation Starter

#OWNYOURPROCESS

We all have a path to follow to find our purpose. Along the way, there will be ups, downs, stops, and detours. We will have mountaintop experiences that bring us joy and happiness, as well as valley experiences that bring us pain and sorrow. Navigating these factors can and will cause us to compare our journeys to others. It may cause us to become discouraged, doubt God, want to give up, take shortcuts, and not embrace the moments necessary to develop our purpose. Every successful person and product goes through a process. No process is alike. You are being uniquely processed for the fulfillment and success of your unique purpose. Don't abort your process, own it.

Thoughts and Reflections

_____

_____

_____

_____

_____

_____

_____

_____

_____

_____

_____

_____

_____

SAY NO NOW OR PAY LATER

Wisdom Nugget

#SAYNONOWORPAYFORITLATER

To protect your emotional, mental, and physical energy, you will sometimes have to say no, even after you've said yes. Don't allow anyone to make you feel as though you don't have the right to say no. Remember, this is not out of selfishness but out of a consciousness of where you are and to preserve your energy. No is a complete sentence, and it does not always require an explanation. Please don't try to justify or over-explain your "no" to people. Sometimes, people only care about how much you can do for them, but never show how much they care and appreciate you. If your desire to embrace self-care is not respected or your care is not reciprocated, it may be time to reconsider some of the tasks you've agreed to do. Saying yes when you should have said no many times can and will leave you physically and emotionally drained.

Thoughts and Reflections

_____

_____

_____

_____

_____

_____

_____

_____

_____

_____

_____

LOL
Devotional

#LOL

"A cheerful heart is good medicine, but a broken spirit saps a person's strength."

Proverbs 17:22 (NLT)

At times in life, it will seem like there is nothing to laugh about. In these moments, we must challenge ourselves to find something that makes us laugh. Laughter is like medicine to the soul. Do you and your friends have weird inside jokes? Does your family have funny stories that you share during family gatherings? Think about one of those instances and allow yourself to laugh. What made you laugh about this particular one? Today, laugh at something and find a way to share a laugh with a friend or co-worker. It's therapeutic! Laughter will make you feel better and bring healing to your soul.

Thoughts and Reflections

_____

_____

_____

_____

_____

_____

_____

_____

_____

_____

_____

CALL ON JESUS

Devotional

#CALLONJESUS

"Call to Me, and I will answer you, and show you great and mighty things, which you do not know.'"

Jeremiah 33:3 (NKJV)

During the day, we hear our names called by people who want to say hello, need something from us, or want our attention. We also call others' names for the same reasons. When we hear our names called, we feel needed. It gives us a sense of value. Today, call on the name that is above every name, which is Jesus (Philippians 2:9). Give His name special attention. There is power, salvation, deliverance, and healing in the name of Jesus. His name is a strong tower we can run to for safety (Proverbs 18:10). Let's not be guilty of calling everybody else's name for answers, comfort, and peace as we leave Jesus' name on the backup list.

Thoughts and Reflections

_____

_____

_____

_____

_____

_____

_____

_____

_____

_____

WEAK MOMENTS
Wisdom Nugget

#ITSOKAYTOHAVEWEAKMOMENTS

Be strong is not always the best advice to give. It's important for people to know that it's okay to have weak moments – even when everyone expects you to be strong. Don't put unrealistic expectations on yourself or others during these difficult times. Jesus, the Son of God, experienced weak moments during His time on Earth. He was God, but He also took on the feelings of man. As a child, one of the first scriptures you were probably taught was, "Jesus wept," (John 11:35 NKJV). In this text, after hearing about the death of His friend, Lazarus, Jesus cried. Also, before His death on the cross, Jesus wept in the Garden of Gethsemane. The agony of what He was destined to do caused Him to struggle mentally and emotionally. Even though He died on the cross for our sins and became Savior of the world, He still had His weak moments. If the Son of God had moments, undoubtedly, you are entitled to have yours as well. The moral of the story is to experience these moments, but don't live in these moments forever.

Thoughts and Reflections

COMMUNICATION

Wisdom Nugget

#HEARTHENONVERBALCOMMUNICATION

Nonverbal communication is one of the most powerful, yet overlooked, forms of communication we use. This is when words and messages are sent through facial expressions, gestures, inactivity, and silence. A person can say one thing verbally and communicate something different non-verbally. Listen for the verbal and non-verbal communication in your relationships. Outweighing one more than the other can lead to an issue of interpreting mixed messages. Listen to both together to hear what's being communicated. This can save you heartache, help you navigate relationship decisions, and possibly save a life. What non-verbal communication have you ignored lately? What non-verbal messages are you sending to the people in your life? Maybe there is a message going unaddressed.

Thoughts and Reflections

_____

_____

_____

_____

_____

_____

_____

_____

_____

_____

_____

_____

_____

ALL IN
Conversation Starter

#HEALTHYVSUNHEALTHYALLIN

Before you decide to be "all in," know that there are two ways to be all in:

A Healthy All In: constitutes a commitment to God first then to others with respect, honor, and sacrifice. You are still able to maintain a balanced life.

An Unhealthy All In: constitutes a commitment to others first then to God. It is fostered and shaped by control, manipulation, and intimidation. You lose the ability to live a balanced life.

Are the relationships or opportunities presented to you or that you are currently in reflecting a healthy or unhealthy all-in? How are you all in?

Thoughts and Reflections

_____

_____

_____

_____

_____

_____

_____

_____

_____

_____

_____

_____

_____

ASSIGNMENTS ONLY

Wisdom Nugget

#ONLYTAKEYOURASSIGNMENTS

People will ask you to complete tasks, be a part of ventures, and lead initiatives on their behalf because of your gifts, talents, and abilities. Proceed with caution. Being gifted and talented to do something does not make it your assignment. When we are naturally gifted and talented in certain areas, we are more prone to say yes to tasks in those areas without reasoning, prayer, and consideration of timing. Saying no to something that is not your assignment doesn't always mean saying never. Don't allow anyone to pressure you to say yes or make you feel guilty for saying no. Ask God to show you where to put your time and energy. Time is too precious to waste on a yes that should have been a no.

Thoughts and Reflections

_____

_____

_____

_____

_____

_____

_____

_____

_____

_____

_____

_____

LOOK IN THE MIRROR
Conversation Starter

#LOOKINTHEMIRROR

Just because we have a right to have an opinion does not mean we should always share it. It's easy to judge someone and say what you wouldn't do when you have not been in their shoes. In turn, if we have been in their shoes before, we should be the most merciful and understanding, not the most judgmental and critical. We all have issues that should keep us in touch with our humanity and frailties. Our problems should help us keep in mind the importance of being introspective when commenting on the success and failures of others. The person we see when we look in the mirror should always keep us in a posture of empathy towards others, not a posture of insensitivity. The desire to use words of criticism and judgment towards others should always be preceded by taking an honest look at the person in the mirror. What you see in the mirror may tell you to keep your comments to yourself.

Thoughts and Reflections

_____

_____

_____

_____

_____

_____

_____

_____

_____

_____

DON'T OVER SPIRITUALIZE

Wisdom Nugget

#DONTOVERSPIRITUALIZE

Habitual cycles and deeply rooted, unresolved emotional issues that continue to hinder progress in life and sabotage relationship systems cannot just be labeled with the classic phrases, "just pray about it, or it's an attack of the enemy." Everything can't be wrapped up in spirituality. Every issue can't be addressed with spiritual counsel alone. Spiritual counsel is great and beneficial in its respective place. However, oftentimes, what we need is a clinically trained, professional counselor. That person can help us raise the hard questions with our past and help us objectively take ownership of our role and participation in our failures and failed relationships that keep anti-progressive cycles present in our lives. We can't afford to over-spiritualize everything at the cost of our mental and emotional health. It's okay to need and seek help from those trained and gifted to clinically care for persons psychologically. God gave them these gifts and our prayer should be that God lead us to the right one.

Thoughts and Reflections

_____

_____

_____

_____

_____

_____

_____

_____

_____

_____

_____

EMOTIONAL ENERGY
Conversation Starter

#DONTWASTEYOUREMOTIONALENERGY

Having and expressing emotions properly is so important. Emotions help us communicate our thoughts and feelings to others, which can be a healthy or unhealthy exchange. One sign that we are having an unhealthy emotional exchange with others is the experience of feeling constantly drained after communicating with or being in the presence of that person. Another sign is experiencing or feeling like you have been on an emotional rollercoaster in your relationship with a person. This is when you go from one extreme to another, up and down with no sense of emotional stability. Consequently, the storage of unhealthy emotions in one's life can lead to the onset of physical illness. A healthy exchange of emotions involves both parties being mutually vested and supportive in sharing the emotional feel of the relationship to benefit and better grow each other. You owe it to yourself and those your life impacts to practice and maintain emotional intelligence. If not, people will leave you emotionally bankrupt. There are some things and people you can't afford to waste your emotional energy on. It's too valuable.

Thoughts and Reflections

_____

_____

_____

_____

_____

_____

_____

_____

COMPLIMENTS

Wisdom Nugget

"Those who flatter their neighbors are spreading nets for their feet."

Proverbs 29:5 (NIV)

Compliments and accolades without substance equal empty words that are full of flattery. It's difficult to walk on a net without stumbling or falling because of the holes. Don't get caught up in receiving or desiring praise from people. Sometimes, flattery can be a trap in disguise to get you off course. Know the difference between genuine compliments and fake ones. Some of the people who praised Jesus crying, "Hosanna!" were the same ones who shouted, "Crucify Him!" (Matthew 21:9, 27:22). At the end of the day, the most important question we must ask ourselves is, "Was God pleased with my actions?" How do you receive and internalize compliments and accolades? When people praise you, do you give the glory to God that He deserves?

Thoughts and Reflections

_____

_____

_____

_____

_____

_____

_____

_____

_____

_____

UNSTOPPABLE FAVOR

Devotional

#GODGIVESUNSTOPPABLEFAVOR

"Joseph found favor in his eyes and became his attendant. Potiphar put him in charge of his household, and he entrusted to his care everything he owned."

Genesis 39:4 (NIV)

When God decides to place His uncommon favor upon your life, He will break the rules just for you. Joseph was wrongly sent to prison after Potiphar's wife falsely accused him of being with her when he actually ran from her attempt to lure him with lust. Sometimes, even in our pursuit to do right, we suffer. God gave Joseph favor with the prison keeper who later entrusted Joseph with managing the prisoners. The Lord was with Joseph, showed him mercy, and promoted him from the pit to the palace (Genesis 39). His brothers, who desired to kill him but failed, had to go back to him for food and financial help during the famine (Genesis 42). No one and no plot can stop God from favoring His chosen.

Thoughts and Reflections

_____

_____

_____

_____

_____

_____

_____

_____

_____

_____

PASS THE TEST

Devotional

#PASSTHEBEINGLIEDONTEST

"God blesses you when people mock you and persecute you and lie about you and say all sorts of evil things against you because you are my followers."

Matthew 5:11 (NLT)

Some people tell lies, but others have a lying spirit. Those with lying spirits take lying to another level. Unfortunately, being lied on is part of the Christian's journey to maturity and growth. Jesus was lied on behind His back and in His face. The scriptures record that there was no guile (deception or underhandedness) found in His heart and God exalted Him (I Peter 2:22-23). You have not passed the "Being Lied On Test" until you have been lied on in your face and behind your back, but still maintained your witness for God. If you never get to tell your side of the story, God knows your side of the story, and that's all that matters. God sees, He knows, and He will avenge you.

Thoughts and Reflections

_____

_____

_____

_____

_____

_____

_____

_____

_____

#PASSTHEBEINGLIEDONTEST

DECISION MAKING 101

Wisdom Nugget

#DECISIONMAKING101

"For by wise counsel you will wage your own war, and in a multitude of counselors there is safety."

Proverbs 24:6 (NKJV)

n life, there are two types of decisions you will have to make: Decisions you and God should make alone, and decisions that you must make with the aid of wise counsel. Pray this simple prayer, "Lord, help me put my decision-making process in the correct category and receive the right counselors into my life." Do you have any pending decisions that you and God need to discuss? Who can you trust to give you wise counsel? Have you applied the wisdom your counselors have given you? One decision can change your life for the rest of your life. Therefore, decide wisely.

Thoughts and Reflections

_____

_____

_____

_____

_____

_____

_____

_____

_____

_____

_____

_____

_____

A PLACE CALLED THERE

Devotional

#GETTOTHERE

"Then the word of the Lord came to him, saying, 'Arise, go to Zarephath, which belongs to Sidon, and dwell there. See, I have commanded a widow to provide for you.'"

I Kings17:8 (NKJV)

We are living in a time and season wherein you cannot just "be somewhere." We must be in the right place at the right time. In I Kings 17 after Elijah proclaimed a drought and went into hiding out of fear, the Lord instructed him to go to specific places at specific times to be sustained. In order to know where our "there place" is we must learn how to listen and ask for God's instructions and not make moves only based on our own intellect and ingenuity. Take a moment right now and pray this simple but powerful prayer, "Lord put me in the right places at the right times." There are places that God is going to instruct you to go where people will be waiting just to be a blessing to you. Your current conditions don't represent your permanent conditions.

Thoughts and Reflections

_____

_____

_____

_____

_____

_____

_____

_____

_____

THE MIRACLE IN YOUR MOUTH

Devotional

#THEREISAMIRACLEINYOURMOUTH

"For she kept saying to herself, 'If only I touch his cloak, I will be healed."

Matthew 9:21 (NET)

There is a miracle in your mouth. You have to say it before you can physically see it. The woman who suffered with an issue of blood for twelve long years spoke her miracle of healing before it manifested. The words she spoke from her mouth created the right atmosphere of belief and expectation. You have this same power. Let your mouth create your miracle. What miracles will be activated because of your words? The same God that gave this woman a miracle because of her faith, is the same God that still works miracles today. Miracles, signs and wonders shall follow them that believe (Mark 16:17-18).

Thoughts and Reflections

_____

_____

_____

_____

_____

_____

_____

_____

_____

_____

_____

_____

_____

THE MINISTRY OF PRESENCE

Wisdom Nugget

#PRACTICETHEMINISTRYOFPRESENCE

It's natural to want to say the right words when others are in times of crisis and celebration. Unfortunately, people often feed off of what we say more than our commitment to "be there." Presence is a very significant, special, and powerful ministry tool. It is needed to build effective relationships. People may not always understand, acknowledge, or want it when it is initially given, but just knowing you were there speaks in volumes and has significant impact. You don't always have to speak. You don't always have to figure out all the right words to say or verbally articulate your feelings during these times. Let your presence do the talking.

Thoughts and Reflections

_____

_____

_____

_____

_____

_____

_____

_____

_____

_____

_____

_____

THE GOODNESS OF THE LORD
Devotional

#ACKNOWLEDGETHEGOODNESSOFTHELORD

"O give thanks unto the Lord; for he is good: because his mercy endureth forever."

Psalms 118:1 (KJV)

This was a call to praise given by the Psalmist David, a man after God's own heart. It pleases the heart of God when we acknowledge and appreciate His goodness. Sometimes in our walk with God, we need a call to praise to remind us of how we should respond to all that the Lord has done for us. The Lord is not good because He always makes us feel good, all of our bills are paid or we have everything we need and want. The Lord is good because His mercy endureth (meaning it is employed for us 365 days of the year to eternity) forever. It is in front of us, behind us and beside us. The mercy of God allows us to get blessings we could never earn with our best efforts. How has the Lord shown you His goodness? Take a moment and give God praise for what He did not allow to happen to you and for how He has kept and preserved your life.

Thoughts and Reflections

_____

_____

_____

_____

_____

_____

_____

_____

#ACKNOWLEDGETHEGOODNESSOFTHELORD

PRAISE THROUGH

Devotional

#PRAISEYOURWAYTHROUGH

"The LORD is my strength and my defense; he has become my salvation. He is my God, and I will praise him, my father's God, and I will exalt him."

Exodus 15:2 (NIV)

If you ever want to get God's attention in your situation, start praising Him. When we praise God, we make Him bigger than our circumstances. Praise helps us see God high and lifted up, seated on His throne, and reigning in His glory with everything under His divine control. When we choose to praise God in spite of how we feel, we invite Him to live, take up residence, and be at home in our midst. He inhabits the praises of His people (Psalm 22:3). The enemy cannot handle a praiser because praise confuses him. He thinks his plots, schemes, and attacks will make us lose our hope for victory. When in actuality for the praiser, these are just cues to turn up the praise and signs that we are closer to our breakthrough. It's time for a praise break. If you handle the praise, God will handle the breakthrough. Praise is a sign that you have won the victory. We must praise God from a place of victory until we get to the place of victory.

Thoughts and Reflections

_____

_____

_____

_____

_____

_____

_____

_____

DELIGHT BEFORE DESIRE

Devotional

#DELIGHTBEFOREDESIRE

"Take delight in the Lord, and he will give you the desires of your heart."

Psalm 37:4 (NIV)

If you delight yourself in the Lord, He will give you the desires of your heart. It's wonderful to know that God wants to give us the desires of our hearts. However, God cannot give us the desires of our hearts until we spend quality time with Him and fall in love with His word and ways. Often, we casually mention the "delight" and put great emphasis on the "desires." You can not have one without the other. The desires of our hearts should flow out of our love for God. Our love for God should purify and qualify the desires of our heart. Sometimes, what we desire does not align with what God desires. The more we fall in love with God, the more our heart and His heart become one. Let's be honest. We don't want good things; we want God's best! The more you delight yourself in God, the more He merges your heart with His heart. Then, the desires of your heart become the desires of His heart for your life.

Thoughts and Reflections

_____

_____

_____

_____

_____

_____

_____

_____

_____

#DELIGHTBEFOREDESIRE

CONTROL & MANIPULATION

Conversation Starter

#CONTROLANDMANIPULATION

Submission should not be requested or demanded through control and manipulation. It should be granted and given because it is warranted from love and respect. What's your thinking on this? Is it okay for someone to use their position and authority to control the minds and actions of others? What does it mean when someone always promises one thing if you do this or that, but they never deliver on the promise (which is a form of bait and switch)? Control and manipulation should not color submission in any relationship. These abusive tactics are used to create fear in relationships and undermine one's ability to think clearly. How are you using your authority in the positions you hold in relationships, at work, or in the church? How would you handle it if you were a victim of control and manipulation?

Thoughts and Reflections

_____

_____

_____

_____

_____

_____

_____

_____

_____

_____

_____

THE POWER OF TOUCH

Wisdom Nugget

#THEPOWEROFTOUCH

There are two types of touch that we can experience: good touch and bad touch. Words are spoken through touch and energy is transferred through touch. Who we touch and who we allow to touch us outwardly (physically) and inwardly (with words) should not be seen as a casual exchange. Set clear and healthy boundaries in these exchanges. Never allow people to become so casual with you that they feel like they can touch you any kind of way. If someone has touched you in a wrong way, it has allowed you to know the difference between good touch and bad touch. Are you purposing to be sensitive and appropriate in the way you touch others with your words and actions? Ultimately, our goal should be to touch someone in a way that positively impacts their life and genuinely makes them feel loved, without any ulterior motives. Take a moment to pray this prayer: "Lord help me to have the right touch with people, identify the wrong touch from people and know when I have experienced a touch from You."

Thoughts and Reflections

_____

_____

_____

_____

_____

_____

_____

_____

_____

CONTROL YOUR THOUGHTS

Devotional

#CONTROLYOURTHOUGHTLIFE

"For as he thinks in his heart, so is he."

Proverbs 23:7 (NKJV)

Every day, thousands of thoughts cross our minds. Some are negative, and some are positive. These thoughts can only take root and live in our minds if we feed them. Our thoughts shape our lives. What we think about the most will show up in our words, actions, and habits. Embrace positive thoughts, and don't feed the negative ones. Our thoughts play a major role in the quality of our life. Have your thoughts negatively impacted the quality of your life? If you had to grade your thought life, what grade would you give yourself? Is there room for improvement? What are some negative thoughts you have been struggling with lately? Take a moment to write down some ways to change these negative thoughts into positive ones.

Thoughts and Reflections

_____

_____

_____

_____

_____

_____

_____

_____

_____

_____

OWN YOUR PART
Conversation Starter

No conflict or crisis in relationships is created in isolation by one party. Each person has played a role whether consciously or subconsciously, intentionally or unintentionally. Sometimes, this role can be as small as not confronting the negative behaviors of others. As easy and seemingly justifiable as it is, we cannot always shift the blame to the offender. We must take ownership of our role, big or small. Yes, it can be humbling and downright humiliating to accept, but at the end of the day, it will help free us from denial, self-righteousness, and unforgiveness. Are there any past or current conflicts in your relationships with others that you failed to own your part in? Take some time to reflect on this question and if applicable, going forward, make the necessary changes.

Thoughts and Reflections

_____

_____

_____

_____

_____

_____

_____

_____

_____

_____

_____

_____

REMEMBER YOUR TESTIMONY
Conversation Starter

#ALWAYSREMEMBERYOURTESTIMONY

"And they overcame him by the blood of the Lamb and by the word of their testimony, and they did not love their lives to the death."

Revelations 12:11 (NKJV)

You are the only one who can testify about what you have experienced in life. Nobody knows your story and all you have had to go through to get where you are right now like you do. Despite the tests and trials sent to discourage you, make you want to quit and maybe even contemplate ending it all, you are still here. God's grace and mercy kept you. You are still here for a reason and purpose bigger than your past and your current circumstances. Take some time right now to remember and reflect on your testimony. Allow it to encourage and strengthen you to keep your faith alive to overcome everything that tries to hinder you from progress. Never forget that your testimony is not just for you, it's for someone else who maybe going through what you survived and needs encouragement and hope. Make a conscious effort to be mindful of the blood of Jesus in your life and rehearse your testimony because together they produce power to defeat the enemy. When was the last time you shared your testimony with someone?

Thoughts and Reflections

_____

_____

_____

_____

_____

_____

OBLIGATIONS & INSPIRATION

Wisdom Nugget

#OBLIGATIONCANKILLINSPIRATION

There should come a time in life when you no longer want to do things out of a sheer obligation only but rather by inspiration. Being unhealthily bound to obligations that are not offering us opportunities to grow and implement our visions and dreams often lead to operating in misplaced loyalties and staying committed to a person or place long after our season is up. When inspiration authentically has the freedom to be birthed and activated, it will lead us to new opportunities and uncharted territory that will bring greater vitality, stability and prosperity. Don't miss your "new thing" by trying to hold on to "old things." "Behold I will do a new thing, now it shall spring forth, shall you not know it? I will even make a road in the wilderness and rivers in the desert," (Isaiah 43:19 NKJV). Authentically find your inspiration and seize it.

Thoughts and Reflections

RAISE YOUR EXPECTATIONS

Conversation Starter

#RAISETHELEVELOFYOUREXPECTATION

"Now to Him who is able to do exceedingly abundantly above all that we ask or think, according to the power that works in us."

Ephesians 3:20 (NKJV)

It's no secret what God can do. What He has done for others, He can do the same for you. God has an unlimited supply of resources to answer the prayers of your wildest dreams. With God, all things are possible (Matthew 19:26). It makes no sense to be in a relationship with a limitless God and put limits on what He can do. What are you expecting God to do in your life? Have you specifically asked Him for what you expect? Take some time now to write down your requests as well as some declarations of your expectations. Expectation is often the breeding ground for miracles!

Thoughts and Reflections

_____

_____

_____

_____

_____

_____

_____

_____

_____

_____

_____

_____

PEOPLE LESSONS

Wisdom Nugget

#PEOPLELESSONS

Sometimes, people are not as bad as others say they are or as good as others say they are. Have you allowed someone to taint the way you treat or interact with someone based on what "they said?" Just because you have a friend that doesn't like someone, they shouldn't expect or try to make you not like the person that they don't like. Get to know a person for yourself and allow them to show you who they are because one day you may be on the other side where people have the choice to believe what, "they said" about you. When God is trying to mature us in some areas, He will send people in our lives with issues and personalities that we don't like or agree with to address our flaws and smooth out some of our rough edges. We are supposed to be God-pleasers, not people-pleasers. You can never please all people and God at the same time.

Thoughts and Reflections

_____

_____

_____

_____

_____

_____

_____

_____

_____

_____

_____

HONESTY BUILDS RELATIONSHIPS

Wisdom Nuggets

#HONESTYBUILDSRELATIONSHIPS

One of the most honorable things you can do in relationships that you value is be straight up and honest. Honesty should be a core value in relationship building. Are you being totally honest in your relationships? Or, are you only telling people what you think they want to hear and showing them what you only want them to see? Everybody wants to be in relationships with people that they can trust. More importantly, trust must be built over time in relationships and the foundation on which it is built is honesty. Where there is only partial honesty, there can only be partial trust.

Thoughts and Reflections

_____

_____

_____

_____

_____

_____

_____

_____

_____

_____

_____

_____

_____

COMMUNICATE
Conversation Starter

One of the most important and healthy things you can do in a relationship that you value is keep the lines of communication open. Lack of communication is the breeding ground for sending wrong messages. Communication is a strong core value necessary in strengthening relationships. Don't stop communicating and get comfortable with shutting down when conflict or misunderstandings arise. Moreover, don't always wait for the other person to initiate the communication, take the lead in the reconciliation. Consequently, you never want someone to get answers from you through assumptions. How can you be a better communicator in your relationships? Are you keeping the lines of communication open in the relationships you value?

Thoughts and Reflections

_____

_____

_____

_____

_____

_____

_____

_____

_____

_____

_____

_____

_____

ACTIONS OVER WORDS

Conversation Starter

#ACTIONSSPEAKLOUDERTHANWORDS

Never go by what people say; go by what their actions tell you. Don't be impressed by words; be informed by actions. It is not the best practice to make a judgment call on a person's character based on an isolated event. Repeated actions reveal patterns in a person's character. When deciding how to define your relationships, take note of the frequency of certain behaviors. Have you unfairly cut someone off because of one action they did without giving them an opportunity to redeem themselves? Or, are you ignoring actions that are red flags? Is it possible that you are avoiding ending certain relationships? In the words of the great late poet and author Maya Angelou, "When people show you who they are, believe them."

Thoughts and Reflections

_____

_____

_____

_____

_____

_____

_____

_____

_____

_____

_____

_____

HEART CONNECTIONS

Wisdom Nugget

#HEARTCONNECTIONS

Change and transition will happen when we least expect it through situations that are extremely painful and difficult to deal with alone. During these times, we must be very sensitive and selective with whom we allow to walk through our transitional seasons with us. At these times, we need what I call "heart connections" to help us heal, recover and advance. A heart connection is a relationship with a person with the sensitivity, grace, empathy, wisdom, knowledge and skill set to help us navigate transitions and provide a safe place for us to confront our pain. In the natural, the heart is one of the most important organs in the body. It pumps blood into our veins and circulatory system to keep us alive. Relationally, heart connections are life-giving agents that will speak and bring life back to what was lost, neglected and buried. Heart connections help us discover what needs to be resolved so that we can progress. Ask God to send and help you identify your heart connections.

Thoughts and Reflections

_____

_____

_____

_____

_____

_____

_____

_____

_____

LET GOD DO IT
Devotional

#LETGODDOIT

"And Moses said to the people, "Do not be afraid. Stand still, and see the salvation of the LORD, which He will accomplish for you today. For the Egyptians whom you see today, you shall see again no more forever."

Exodus 14:13 (NKJV)

God is the best defense attorney and vindicator. He sees and knows all things. We often say, "Won't He do it?" However, directly following this question should be the contingency, "If you let Him." Sometimes we are guilty of being in our own way which can hinder our progress and blessings. Get out of God's way, stay prayed up, and turn your situation over to God. Then, sit back and watch Him work on your behalf. When it seems like our enemies are getting the best of us, it can be challenging to relinquish the power in our hands so God can reveal the power in His mighty hands. These are the times we must remember that God wants to fight for us, but we have to let Him. Yes, you are strong and smart. But God is stronger and wiser. Don't waste your energy and time on something only God can do. He will even make your enemies your footstool (Psalm 110:1).

Thoughts and Reflections

_____

_____

_____

_____

_____

_____

_____

DELIVERANCE 101

Wisdom Nugget

#DELIVERANCE101

"Stand fast therefore in the liberty by which Christ has made us free, and do not be entangled again with a yoke of bondage."

Galatians 5:1 (KJV)

The people we spend the most time with can have the greatest influence on our character. If you are trying to get delivered from something (or have been delivered from something), do not hang around people who are struggling with that same issue. There is a difference between sharing your time with someone and sharing your testimony with someone. Once deliverance has been received in an area of our lives, we must protect and fill that area of our lives with the right behaviors, accountability and positive reinforcements. It has been proven that we become products of our environment. We must keep ourselves in environments that cultivate restoration, not relapse.

Thoughts and Reflections

_____

_____

_____

_____

_____

_____

_____

_____

_____

_____

LOVE

Wisdom Nugget

#LOVE

Love does not take advantage of another person. Instead, it is a source of strength in their weaknesses. Love should not function like a light switch that can be turned on and off. It should be freely given and consistently shown through a mutual exchange of corresponding actions – not just words alone. Love should not keep score, seek to get even, or create its own glory. Love should be reciprocated, factor in sacrifice, and receive unsolicited praise. "Love is patient, love is kind. It does not envy, it does not boast, it is not proud. It does not dishonor others, it is not self-seeking, it is not easily angered, it keeps no record of wrongs (I Corinthians 13:4-5 NIV)." In this scripture passage, the Apostle Paul gives us the template definition of the love we deserve and should embody in relationships. Are you receiving and demonstrating this type of love? What do you know and believe about love?

Thoughts and Reflections

_____

_____

_____

_____

_____

_____

_____

_____

_____

_____

_____

_____

APPLY WHAT YOU LEARN

Wisdom Nugget

#APPLYWHATYOULEARN

Valuable information must lead to application. Don't spend time and money learning life-changing information that you never apply to your life. When you invest in yourself, you owe it to yourself to use what you've learned. Because of God's spiritual investment in you, you also owe it to Him to apply what you know. The college degrees, certifications, trainings, seminars, coaching, biblical knowledge or wise counsel you have received has afforded you invaluable information. The application of valuable information can lead to an opportunity of a lifetime, the fulfillment of your dreams, unlimited wealth, and making a difference in the lives of others. English Philosopher Francis Bacon said, "knowledge is power." I would like to take it a step further and say, "applied knowledge is power." What are you doing with all the information and knowledge you have gained over the years? Search and analyze your arsenal of information because you could be sitting on a goldmine and not know it.

Thoughts and Reflections

_____

_____

_____

_____

_____

_____

_____

_____

_____

_____

#APPLYWHATYOULEARN

LIVE MORE
Wisdom Nugget

#YOUDESERVETOLIVEMORE

When was the last time you did something special for yourself? Don't spend your life only investing in others. You deserve to live too. What sense does it make to work forty to fifty hours a week for someone else, but never pay yourself? Never be so busy for others that you forget that you need you as well. Yes, life is supposed to be shared with others, but this should never be at the expense of your self-care. Make your happiness a priority. Life is a gift from God. As receivers of this gift, we should choose to unwrap it each day and live it to the fullest. It's time for you to live more. What are three ways that you can do something special for yourself that you have not done in a long time or never done before? Now, put dates on these three things that will allow you to plan and make them happen over the next three to six months.

Thoughts and Reflections

_____

_____

_____

_____

_____

_____

_____

_____

_____

_____

_____

_____

ISSA COMEBACK

Devotional

#ISSACOMEBACK

"Now thanks be to God who always leads us in triumph in Christ, and through us diffuses the fragrance of His knowledge in every place."

II Corinthians 2:14 (NKJV)

We will all make decisions that may cause us to experience embarrassment, setbacks, and even failure. Ultimately, these experiences will help us become better equipped to live in and on purpose. Oftentimes, after difficult losses, we struggle to regain our confidence to try again. Despite what we have gone through, we must build up the confidence to try again. Struggle will often cost you shame and embarrassment on the front end, but provide you endurance on the back end for one of the greatest comebacks of your life. Don't despise failure. Failures position you to be stronger, wiser, and better. What's coming to you is going to be so much better than what's been.

Thoughts and Reflections

_____

_____

_____

_____

_____

_____

_____

_____

_____

_____

_____

RELATIONSHIP MANAGEMENT

Conversation Starter

#RELATIONSHIPMANAGEMENT

Managing relationships requires commitment, patience, and flexibility. Moreover, in relationships we must be careful not to judge people off of one isolated event that happens. Yes, maybe they did have an off day. It's very possible that they missed the mark or dropped the ball. However, don't forget about the many times they came through for you. It takes discernment to know the difference between an action that warrants termination or reconciliation. Also, in some cases, in order for a relationship to get better and be appreciated, it requires some time apart, some distance. In Proverbs 13:12 (NKJV), Solomon gives us this wisdom, "Hope deferred makes the heart sick, but when the desire comes, it is a tree of life." Sometimes, we have to disconnect to reconnect. Then there are times when God ends a thing and closes the door.

Thoughts and Reflections

_____

_____

_____

_____

_____

_____

_____

_____

_____

_____

_____

_____

DON'T ABUSE GRACE

Devotional

#DONTABUSEGRACE

Experiencing and receiving grace from God and others is beautiful and honorable. However, no one wants the grace they extend to be taken for granted or abused. When we give people chance after chance to get something right, there is an expectation for improvement or accuracy. So it is with God. Unfortunately, grace is often seen through a lens that highlights grace but dims accountability. As a result, grace is more likely to be abused in situations that breed and recruit cosigners instead of welcoming and wanting analyzers. When I seek counsel or vent with my friends about my issues, I always tell them "I'm not looking for cosigners. Tell me where I'm wrong!" Then we discuss ways that I can do better and work to get it right. Grace from God denotes that He will cover you while you work to get it right not, He will cover you while you continue to consciously get it wrong with no intentions to change. It is more honorable for us to be seen struggling and fighting for change than to be seen unconvicted and unbothered to change. The Apostle Paul makes this clear for us in Romans 6:1-6 and Philippians 2:12-13. It is such a privilege and honor to have God's grace at work in our lives. How are you handling and valuing His grace?

Thoughts and Reflections

_____

_____

_____

_____

_____

_____

_____

_____

UNDERSTAND RELATIONSHIPS

Conversation Starter

#UNDERSTANDRELATIONSHIPS

At times in relationships, you have to agree to disagree and be willing to see things from the other person's view. This is good because seeing things from a different perspective gives room for great dialogue that often leads to an even greater understanding of others. If we always have a problem with others disagreeing with us and deny them the freedom to express their views, we close one of the greatest bridges to building healthy relationships. In order to be successful, relationships must place getting understanding over being domineering. When you are willing to get an understanding of the other person's side, it means you are willing to come under their stance. In order for this to happen, you must lower your desire to prove your point and put yourself in their shoes for a moment. It's called empathy, to feel with, not to make them feel like you.

Thoughts and Reflections

_____

_____

_____

_____

_____

_____

_____

_____

_____

_____

_____

EXPIRATION DATES

Wisdom Nugget

#HONORTHEEXPIRATIONDATE

People come into our lives for reasons, seasons, or a lifetime. We must know the difference. Once we understand this, we may have to give up things and people we believe are good, in order for us to obtain God's best for us. Don't keep anyone or anything in your life past their expiration date. Once food expires, it spoils. If we eat spoiled food, we could possibly get food poisoning. If we keep things and people in our lives past their expiration dates, they can contaminate our mind, spirit, and body. Are you holding on to something or someone that you should have let go? Don't be so quick to answer. Sit with this question a few days, give it great thought, and then come back to this page and respond.

Thoughts and Reflections

_____

_____

_____

_____

_____

_____

_____

_____

_____

_____

_____

_____

_____

#HONORTHEEXPIRATIONDATE

THE RIGHT SUPPORT

Wisdom Nugget

#GETTHERIGHTSUPPORT

There is a difference between right and wrong support. The right support causes us to be progressive and productive, while the wrong support causes us to be stagnant and digressive. Have you ever seen a person who depends on someone else to be there for them and grow with them, but all that person does is keep them in the same place doing the same things? Better yet, have you experienced a time when the company you kept influenced you to think small? When we look at our support system, we should see more people who represent where we need to be and not mostly people who represent where we are right now. Do you have the right support in your life? Do you have the right team pushing your vision? If not, what support do you need and what gifts do you need on your team? Take some time right now and turn those needs into a prayer to God.

Thoughts and Reflections

_____

_____

_____

_____

_____

_____

_____

_____

_____

_____

_____

_____

#GETTHERIGHTSUPPORT

REPENT & FORGIVE

Devotional

#REPENTANDFORGIVE

"Bear with each other and forgive one another if any of you has a grievance against someone. Forgive as the Lord forgave you."

Colossians 3:13 (NIV)

After we have been wronged and hurt by others, it can be difficult to forgive and the last thing we may feel we need to do is repent. What may we need to repent for? We may need to repent for holding on to anger, wanting to get even, unforgiveness and the unspoken words said in our minds and hearts against them that do not please God. Forgiveness is a two-way street with God. We cannot expect forgiveness from God and others and not freely give it ourselves. If you know that you are harboring unforgiveness or holding a grudge against someone, repent now and ask for forgiveness from God and if necessary, the person as well. Harboring unforgiveness and anger is the perfect recipe for self-destruction. Forgiveness is a choice, not a feeling. It's not easy but it is necessary to please God. The longer we wait to repent and forgive, the longer our healing, deliverance and peace will remain incomplete.

Thoughts and Reflections

_____

_____

_____

_____

_____

_____

_____

QUALITY FRIENDS
Wisdom Nugget

Some people are consumed with having so many people to call friend in life and obtaining thousands of followers on social media because they believe that the more friends and followers you have, the more influence, exposure, and support you have. Is this a realistic measurement? Unfortunately, this same mindset often colors the way a person perceives the ethics of friendship. What good is it to have hundreds of friends without the qualifications for friendship like honesty, dependability, mutuality, empathy, and accountability? When was the last time the people you consider friends impacted your life for the better, challenged you to grow, showed compassion towards you, took time to appreciate you, or demonstrated leadership to you? In life, friendships should never be about quantity but rather, quality.

Thoughts and Reflections

_____

_____

_____

_____

_____

_____

_____

_____

_____

_____

_____

WOUNDED HEALERS

Wisdom Nugget

#WOUNDEDHEALERS

In serving others and God wholeheartedly, it's easy for us to become wounded healers due to suffering repeated losses, experiencing major disappointments, and the insensitivities of others. During these times when we ourselves need healing or a time to grieve, God will use us to heal others. This is often a test of commitment and character building wherein the teacher is silent. Though the teacher is silent, He is watching us. He has graced us for the tasks at hand and will in time allow our healing to manifest too. It can be very painful to be tasked with duties that require us to help others while we are hurting the most. Ironically, a wound often hurts the most before it heals the most. The blessing, consolation, and reward of being a wounded healer is knowing that the story and message behind your wounds can become the cure for someone else's healing.

Thoughts and Reflections

_____

_____

_____

_____

_____

_____

_____

_____

_____

_____

_____

_____

HOLD YOUR RESPONSE

Wisdom Nugget

#HOLDYOURRESPONSE

When someone says or does something unbelievable, offensive or just flat out wrong, sometimes you have to hold your response. It is not always good or wise to immediately respond. Why? Simply because the initial response in these types of situations tends to be less tempered, more emotional and very reactive instead of controlled, objective and peacemaking. Some people will say and do things to you just to get a response that will bring your character into question. Don't give them that much power. You will often find, in waiting to respond, key elements to the way you should respond and make pending decisions will be revealed. Get clear and controlled in your thinking before you respond. Choose to respond in a way that shows the epitome of your character rather than the height of your frustration.

Thoughts and Reflections

_____

_____

_____

_____

_____

_____

_____

_____

_____

_____

_____

INVEST IN YOURSELF

Wisdom Nugget

#INVESTINYOURSELF

We must understand our value to God and our self-worth (John 3:16). Do you have any clue how valuable you are to God? He gave His only Son so that you could receive salvation. No cost can be attached to His sacrifice. This demonstration of value from God gives us a frame of reference for how we should value ourselves. Have you established what you are worth? How will you protect your worth? What are you willing to invest in your worth? People will measure your worth by how much you value it. Don't be guilty of going through life investing in everybody else's worth and never taking the time to invest in your own. Go back to school. Get those certifications. Take that vacation. Buy the car you deserve. Don't pay rent all your life. Become a homeowner. Start your own business! You are worth the investment.

Thoughts and Reflections

_____

_____

_____

_____

_____

_____

_____

_____

_____

_____

_____

I AM NOT MY MISTAKES

Devotional

#IAMNOTMYMISTAKES

In our humanity (specifically in our immaturity and selfishness), it can be easy to feel like we haven't made any progress toward our purpose and destiny. We can easily become concerned about who believes in us, wants us, accepts us, picks us, or likes our social media statuses. Honestly, the only approval we should be concerned about is God's approval. Unfortunately, sometimes we allow the word curses and opinions of others about our mistakes and past to be on repeat in our minds and negatively color the way we see our worth and progress. Never overlook or underestimate the value of the lessons God taught you through your mistakes and bad choices. These lessons are His investment in your success. God uses our experiences to strategically reveal and develop our purpose and destiny before He fully manifests them through us. Your mistakes from your past don't have to dictate your future (Romans 8:28).

Thoughts and Reflections

_____

_____

_____

_____

_____

_____

_____

_____

_____

_____

GOD QUALIFIES

Devotional

#GODQUALIFIES

"'I knew you before I formed you in your mother's womb. Before you were born, I set you apart and appointed you as my prophet to the nations.' 'O Sovereign Lord,' I said, 'I can't speak for you! I'm too young!' The Lord replied, 'Don't say, 'I'm too young,' for you must go wherever I send you and say whatever I tell you. And don't be afraid of the people, for I will be with you and will protect you. I, the Lord, have spoken!'"

Jeremiah 1: 5-8 (NLT)

One of the greatest silent frustrations of many people is the inability to find or accept their purpose. Many feel unworthy to fulfill and be successful in their purpose because they don't feel qualified. Oftentimes, unbeknownst to us, our God-given purpose that we are searching for and fearful to accept has been at work in us all along. It is not our job to qualify ourselves for purpose. However, it is our job to avail ourselves to the process of walking in purpose. When we avail ourselves to this process, God will ensure that we have experiences in life to prepare us with the necessary qualifications.

Thoughts and Reflections

_____

_____

_____

_____

_____

_____

_____

GOD'S CHOICE
Devotional

#GODSCHOICEWINS

"Philip found Nathanael and said to him, "We have found Him of whom Moses in the law, and the prophets, wrote—Jesus of Nazareth, the son of Joseph."And Nathanael said to him, "Can anything good come out of Nazareth?" Philip said to him, "Come and see."

John 1:45 - 46 (NKJV)

Where we come from does not have to determine where we will go. What we are ashamed of from our past can't stop where God has pre-destined us to go. God specializes in bringing something good out of every bad situation. Our Lord and Savior Jesus knew this firsthand. Mary and Joseph, Jesus' earthly parents who were from Nazareth, were considered poor. To be referred to as a Nazarene meant they were despised. In other words, out of all the places the mother of Jesus could come from, Nazareth was not considered one worthy of such an honor. Nathaniel questioned Jesus' validity asking, "Can anything good come out of Nazareth?" Many don't realize that one's purpose, destiny and anointing are often birthed out of our greatest place of shame, pain, and rejection. God's sovereign choice will always win over human acceptance.

Thoughts and Reflections

_____

_____

_____

_____

_____

_____

GOD'S ANNOUNCEMENT
Devotional

#LISTENFORGODSANNOUNCEMENT

"You will conceive and give birth to a son, and you will name him Jesus. He will be very great and will be called the Son of the Most High. The Lord God will give him the throne of his ancestor David."

Luke 1:31-32 (NLT)

God announces His will for our lives before we fully accept and understand it. God has never called perfect people. He desires to use those who will allow Him to perfect those things that concern them (Psalm 138:8). Before Mary was pregnant with Jesus, the angel came to announce it to her. Mary's initial response was one of doubt and fear. She did not understand how God could do this through her. No matter how inadequate you may feel, God has chosen and created you for a purpose that's bigger than how you perceive yourself. He has already announced greatness over your life! Let's honor His announcement by striving daily to live up to His expectations. Listen for God's announcement over your life. It will always call you to greatness and never allow you to settle for mediocrity.

Thoughts and Reflections

_____

_____

_____

_____

_____

_____

_____

_____

WHAT YOU CALL IT MATTERS

Devotional

#WHATYOUCALLITMATTERS

"Out of the ground the Lord God formed every beast of the field and every bird of the air, and brought them to Adam to see what he would call them. And whatever Adam called each living creature, that was its name."

Genesis 2:19 (NKJV)

While we are wanting and many times fighting to embrace God's will for our lives and our family's lives, we must make sure that we are calling our situations and purpose what God is calling them. Words have creative power. Names are powerful and must be used with care and caution. In Genesis, what I like to call, "The Call It Law," was established. Adam demonstrates for us the power of calling things how they will become identified. Even when you don't have any tangible evidence that you are going to give birth to your purpose, you have to call those things that are not, as though they were, by faith. Your words must become hope-filled even when your situation looks hopeless. What are you calling your purpose and speaking over your situations? What are you naming your vision while it is in seed-form?

Thoughts and Reflections

_____

_____

_____

_____

_____

_____

_____

DON'T WORRY ABOUT THE HOW

Devotional

#DONTWORRYABOUTTHEHOW

"For God is working in you, giving you the desire and the power to do what pleases him."

Philippians 2:13 (NLT)

While we are becoming the person God wants us to be as we walk into our destiny and purpose, there is often a tendency to put more emphasis on how it is going to happen than who is going to make it happen. What God is going to do through you is more important than how He is going to do it. Once God chooses to start a work in us, He is faithful to produce the finished product through our obedience. This is why the Apostle Paul once known as Saul, a persecutor of the church who called himself, "the chief of sinners," could proclaim "being confident of this very thing, that He who has begun a good work in you will complete it until the day of Jesus Christ (Philippians 1:6). Our responsibility is to embrace and trust the process, not control it.

Thoughts and Reflections

_____

_____

_____

_____

_____

_____

_____

_____

_____

TIMING IS EVERYTHING
Devotional

#TIMINGISEVERYTHING

"To everything there is a season, a time for every purpose under heaven."

Ecclesiastes 3:1 (NKJV)

When is it going to be my turn? When will it all make sense? Will things ever change? When raising these questions to God, it's possible that our timing is not in alignment with His timing. God has an appointed time and due season to bring us into the fullness of our purpose and vision. He exemplifies this for us through Jesus. Galatians 4:4-5(NKJV), states, "But when the fullness of time had come, God sent His son, born of a woman, born under the law, to redeem those who were under the law, that we might receive the adoption as sons." Our becoming processes are not a part of a contest. They are personalized journeys, orchestrated and navigated by God to ensure that we have all the necessary tools like character, integrity, patience, wisdom and faith to handle and carry out the tasks aligned with our purpose. Take a moment to write some positive statements to confess that reinforce your trust in God's timing for the things you're believing to come to pass in your life.

Thoughts and Reflections

_____

_____

_____

_____

_____

_____

DECLARATIONS
Devotional

"You will also declare a thing, and it will be established for you; so light will shine on your ways."

Job 22:28 (NKJV)

Making positive declarations is key to building your faith and establishing a healthy mindset. Declaration always precedes manifestation. Make this declaration: "My times are in the hands of the Lord. I cannot control God's timing. He knows what is best for me and who is best for me. Delay does not mean denial. Delays are God's protection. Today, I take my hands off every situation and circumstance that has frustrated me because of impatience, worry, and fear of being behind schedule or too late. Holy Spirit, help me to know God's timing, and sharpen my discernment. I will not run ahead of God to satisfy my flesh. I submit my life to God's timetable.I have peace and assurance that God is in control, and He has appointed a time to bring me into the fullness of my purpose. I will not abort my process. Giving up is not an option. God has already seen my end from the beginning and declared greatness over my life. Therefore, I will walk in obedience, faith, and expectation."

Thoughts and Reflections

_____

_____

_____

_____

_____

_____

_____

_____

GOD REROUTED YOU

Wisdom Nugget

#GODREROUTEDYOU

Have you ever believed something would happen in your life a certain way so strongly that there was no doubt in your mind that it could happen another way? Then, when you least expected it, the whole way you believed it was supposed to happen blew completely up? This can be very mind-boggling and heart-breaking to us, yet God-ordained. God often uses the confusion, pain and struggle of a setback to get us on the right track. Are you wondering why it did not happen the way you thought it would with the relationship, job, children, business deal, house search, transition or vision? God was rerouting you so that you would make the necessary stops and turns to ensure that you will arrive at the destinations He planned for your life. Thank God that He rerouted you then so that you would not be lost later. "It's not how fast you get to a destination that matters most. Direction should be paramount to speed."- Pastor Spencer T. O'neal.

Thoughts and Reflections

_____

_____

_____

_____

_____

_____

_____

_____

_____

THE STRENGTH EXCHANGE
Devotional

"And He said to me, "My grace is sufficient for you, for My strength is made perfect in weakness." Therefore most gladly I will rather boast in my infirmities, that the power of Christ may rest upon me."

II Corinthians 12:9 (NKJV)

It is easy to attempt, yet unwise to believe that we can overcome and accomplish things solely in our own strength. Whenever we believe we don't need anybody's help, we can become intellectually and emotionally independent to a fault. I know we live in a world that promotes independence, but we must be careful not to negate our dependence on God. Our physical strength can't equate to the power of God's spiritual strength that is accessible to us. In II Corinthians 12:8, the Apostle Paul asked God three times to remove the thorn (his weakness or issue) in his flesh. Paul was a gifted servant of God, but he still had an issue that kept him on his knees in prayer. Like Paul, we must humble ourselves and accept the strength God has made available to us. God won't always immediately remove the weakness or issue we face in life when we pray, but He will help us to overcome them through grace to develop and mature us. Don't try to physically and mentally overcompensate for things that can only be achieved through the strength and grace of God.

Thoughts and Reflections

ATMOSPHERE CHANGERS
Devotional

#ATMOSPHERECHANGERS

Have you ever walked into a place or situation and felt energy or an aura that impacted your spirit and emotions? It's called an atmosphere - the influencing tone, mood or air of a particular place. Atmospheres are created by what people hear, say, think, and do. It is important that we take an active and intentional role in creating the right atmospheres and changing or exiting the wrong atmospheres. Atmosphere Changers face their fears. They don't try to fit in; they position themselves for impact. Atmosphere Changers believe God and His prophets and practice prophetic praise. We see all of these characteristics exemplified in II Chronicles 20:14-22, when three enemy nations surrounded King Jehoshaphat and the people of Judah. After praying and fasting before the Lord, God used the Levite Jahaziel to give a prophetic word proclaiming victory. They believed his word and did not conform to the carnal weapons of war. They positioned themselves for victory and praised God before it happened. In this atmosphere, the enemies that sought to kill them killed each other. You have the power to be an Atmosphere Changer. Are you making a conscious effort daily to create the right atmospheres in your life?

Thoughts and Reflections

_____

_____

_____

_____

_____

_____

DISCORD SOWERS

Wisdom Nugget

#BEWAREOFDISCORDSOWERS

At best, our conversations with family, friends, and people we meet in our everyday lives should be mutually rewarding, positive, worthwhile, and productive. In some cases, this requires a filtering process to keep the exchange of words pure and peaceful. Anytime someone makes it their business to stir up conflict, paint a negative picture of others, or oppose truth, division and disagreements will occur. These individuals are called Discord Sowers. Discord is disagreement or a lack of harmony between people. Discord Sowers must be directly stopped. Don't allow them to have free reign with you. The more you listen to them, the more you will become contaminated with bad energy, thoughts, and feelings about a person or situation. This can unnecessarily and prematurely cause you to lose friendships, destroy relationships, and judge wrongly. Are there any Discord Sowers in your life that you need to address, disconnect from, or repent to God about?

Thoughts and Reflections

_____

_____

_____

_____

_____

_____

_____

_____

_____

PEOPLE HURT AND HEAL

Wisdom Nugget

#PEOPLEHURTANDHEALYOU

Some of our greatest hurts come from people, but some of our greatest healings come through people. People may purpose to hurt you but God purposes to use people to heal you. What one person tried to kill in you, God will use another person to bring back to life. Don't allow what some people have done to you cause you to give up on believing in the good God has placed on the inside of so many people to be a blessing to you. Expect God to send people in your life to re-ignite your dreams, support your visions, rebuild your self-confidence and renew your smile. Where are you in your healing process from people that hurt you? Is there someone you know you have been assigned by God to help heal but have not embraced yet? If you've been healed from hurtful things done to you by others, share your testimony with someone who you know needs to hear it.

Thoughts and Reflections

WE TEACH PEOPLE

Conversation Starter

We teach people how to treat us by what we allow. Don't allow what should not happen to you become normal for you to accept from people. Once you normalize wrong behavior, it gets worse. How are you teaching people to treat you? Are there some things you need to change and adjust about your actions and personality that has often sent the wrong message to people about what you are okay with in your relationships? Once people get comfortable with addressing and handling you a certain way in relationships, it makes it more difficult for you to change the dynamics of the relationship to fit expectations you never voiced and explained. Do you have any re-teaching to do in your relationships? If so, how do you plan to approach it? More importantly, be mindful that the only way your re-teaching will be successful is if the person will listen and be willing to make the necessary changes to treat you better.

Thoughts and Reflections

_____

_____

_____

_____

_____

_____

_____

_____

_____

_____

_____

INCONVENIENCES SAVE LIVES

Devotional

#INCONVENIENCESSAVELIVES

I t can be extremely frustrating when we have to do things that we did not plan on doing or wait for things we believed and expected to happen by a certain time. In these moments, we can easily get irritated, blame others, and stop believing for the best. Understand that if God stopped it or blocked it, He did it for a good reason. Don't allow the enemy to frustrate, torment, accuse, or vex you just because it has not happened yet. Joseph, who was favored by God, had a dream of his success and shared it with his brothers. Out of jealousy, his brothers attempted to kill him. They threw him in a pit, and he was sold as a slave to serve in Potiphar's house. However, it was his service there that led him to the palace and secured him a prestigious position to save his family. Joseph was inconvenienced and delayed, but not denied. Sometimes what inconveniences us for a moment will save us and others a lifetime. After Joseph went through these very trying times, he was able to say these words: "You intended to harm me, but God intended it all for good. He brought me to this position, so I could save the lives of many people," (Genesis 50:20 NLT).

Thoughts and Reflections

_____

_____

_____

_____

_____

_____

_____

THE MINISTRY OF MISTAKES
Conversation Starter

#THEMINISTRYOFMISTAKES

M aking mistakes doesn't feel good. However, our mistakes can work for our good if we choose to learn from them. Our mistakes serve as lessons in the classroom of life. There are no perfect people in the world. Everyone makes mistakes – even the people you admire. Don't be hard on yourself when you make a mistake. Let your goal be to not make the same mistakes over and over again with no signs of growth or change. The lessons we learn from our mistakes give us the wisdom and knowledge to prevent us from making the same mistakes. Every day, people all over the world use their mistakes to find solutions to problems, start businesses, create positive change, and encourage others. You can be one of these people too. It's called the ministry of mistakes. What is one of the greatest lessons in your life that you learned from a mistake you made?

Thoughts and Reflections

_____

_____

_____

_____

_____

_____

_____

_____

_____

_____

THE POWER OF CONTEXT
Conversation Starter

#THEPOWEROFCONTEXT

Have you ever experienced someone misunderstanding something you said or did because they used an isolated statement or incident to draw conclusions? This often happens when people do not base their understanding on knowing the entire context of your words and actions. Truth and understanding are best perceived and heard when the principle of context is applied. Context is everything surrounding the setting of a statement or incident so that it can be fully understood and assessed. Never underestimate the power of context in communication, decision-making and conflict-resolution. It allows us to see and hear beyond the surface. Don't be guilty of judging matters in isolation void of context, get the context first, then proceed. Do you have any pending decisions that you need to get more context to make? Are there any apologies you need to make to some people because you failed to get proper context?

Thoughts and Reflections

_____

_____

_____

_____

_____

_____

_____

_____

_____

_____

HEALTHY RELATIONSHIPS
Conversation Starter

#CREATEHEALTHYRELATIONSHIPS

Sometimes God allows friction, confusion and disputes in relationships that are worth your investment to destroy unhealthy boundaries and set clear healthy boundaries. Some relationships just need to be realigned and reconstructed, not ended. Strong relationships are built as a result of being clearly defined. Whatever we expect in relationships, we must be willing to give. Relationships are hinged on communication, reciprocity and appreciation. What are the core values that form your relationship boundaries? What are those boundaries and how do you know when you have allowed your relationships to go outside of those boundaries? Are you giving as much as you are asking for? Have you consistently shown in words and deeds how much you appreciate your friends and family? How well are those you are in relationship with giving back to you? Can you honestly and confidently say that there is a mutual sacrifice? If not, how can you all begin to make the relationships healthier?

Thoughts and Reflections

_____

_____

_____

_____

_____

_____

_____

_____

_____

KNOW THYSELF

Wisdom Nugget

#KNOWTHYSELF

How well do you know yourself? Are you aware of your weaknesses and your strengths? What makes you happy? What is your God-given passion that will make a difference in the lives of others? What do you really need in a relationship? From a health perspective, are you in touch with your body? What are your favorite things? What is your dream vacation? What is your credit score? Are you practicing financially sound principles? What are your short-term and long-term goals? What do you need to do to achieve those goals? Are you in a healthy place emotionally and spiritually? Are you harboring any anger or unforgiveness? All these questions are essential to you truly knowing who you are, what you need, what you don't need, and what is best for you. So many people go through life getting to know hundreds and thousands of people, places, and things, yet fail to get to know the person in the mirror. Having self-awareness is tremendously essential to creating and experiencing your best life.

Thoughts and Reflections

_____

_____

_____

_____

_____

_____

_____

_____

_____

#KNOWTHYSELF

WORK YOUR FAITH

Devotional

#WORKYOURFAITH

"Now faith is the substance of things hoped for, the evidence of things not seen."

Hebrews 11:1 (NKJV)

At times, we put more emphasis on having faith in words instead of working our faith with actions. The Bible tells us that faith without works is dead, (James 2:17). In our walk with God, we won't always see our way in the natural and our faith steps cannot be based on our five senses. You won't always feel or see God moving. In our finite minds we cannot figure God out. We have to trust Him, which is often a blind trust. When you work your faith, you must see the invisible. Faith takes steps in the dark believing and knowing that the lights will come on in the journey. Workers of faith don't major on the tangibles, but rather they thrive on and embrace the intangibles, the possibilities, the risks and the what ifs. What are you waiting on? It's time for you to do what you said and see what you saw. Take the leap, work your faith past the last level you used it on and watch your vision become a reality.

Thoughts and Reflections

_____

_____

_____

_____

_____

_____

_____

GOD IS WORKING

Wisdom Nugget

#GODISWORKINGBEHINDTHESCENES

Our blessings are often connected to conflict or on the other side of a conflicting situation. The conflict is just a smokescreen. God is working behind the scenes on your behalf. He is orchestrating scenes and writing the script. In the end, it will all make sense. A good movie or book has moments of suspense and a twist in the storyline that makes the viewer or reader nervous and filled with great anticipation at the same time. The character that seems to be taking a turn for the worse will all of a sudden overtake the villain. The storyline of your life may have you in a place of uncertainty, anxiousness or fear, but don't let it kill your anticipation. What's coming is better than what's been! Don't miss your blessing because you don't like the package that it is coming in. Stay the course because God is working behind the scenes of your life on blessings designed just for you!

Thoughts and Reflections

_____

_____

_____

_____

_____

_____

_____

_____

_____

_____

ACCEPT THE UPGRADE
Conversation Starter

#ACCEPTTHEUPGRADE

One day, someone damaged my car. As my insurance company took care of the repairs, I had to use a rental car. When I arrived to pick up my rental, I was informed that they didn't have any more cars that were compatible with my vehicle, but would give me an upgrade. I had many apprehensions because of the size of the upgraded rental. Unfortunately, the only other car the company could offer me was a downgrade of the car that had initially been reserved for me. I did not want that car either. For about ten minutes, I sat in the upgraded rental to see if I could handle it. I made every excuse as to why I could not take this upgraded car and how uncomfortable it made me feel. Right then and there, the Holy Spirit said to me, "Accept the upgrade." I quickly made the mental and emotional adjustments to accept what God had strategically and lovingly given to me. God always wants the best for us. Where is God trying to upgrade you? Are you resisting the upgrade because you are settling for what you are used to? Don't miss your upgrade because it doesn't feel right. Don't miss your upgrade because you don't feel prepared for it. Don't miss your upgrade because you think it's coming at the wrong time.

Thoughts and Reflections

_____

_____

_____

_____

_____

_____

ANTICIPATE ANGELS
Devotional

#ANTICIPATEANGELS

"Don't forget to show hospitality to strangers, for some who have done this have entertained angels without realizing it!"

Hebrews 13:2 (NLT)

The ministry of angels is one of the most underestimated ministries, primarily because many don't understand it. God never intended for this ministry to be looked at as something spooky or that we should fear. Yes, there are evil spirits in the world perpetrating as good spirits. Even the devil is described in the Bible as one who "masquerades as an angel of light," whose purpose is to deceive (II Corinthians 11:14 NIV). However, God's angels are ministering spirits He assigns to us in the earth realm to communicate the will of God, execute the purposes and judgments of God, and strengthen and encourage the children of God. There are several events recorded in scripture, where God used angels to help people. In Acts 12:5-10, when Peter was wrongly imprisoned, the church prayed for him fervently. An angel came into his jail cell, shined a light on him, and said, "Arise quickly." Peter's chains fell off his hands, and the angel led him to freedom. Anticipate God sending angels to encourage you, strengthen you, direct you, and intervene for you in situations that seem to be over and have no hope. Pray that your eyes and heart be open to the angels assigned to your life.

Thoughts and Reflections

_____

_____

_____

_____

_____

YOU CAN BEGIN AGAIN
Devotional

#YOUCANBEGINAGAIN

"After Job had prayed for his friends, the LORD restored his fortunes and gave him twice as much as he had before."

Job 42:10 (NIV)

The thought of starting over can be disheartening, dreading and oftentimes daring at the same time. Disheartening because of feeling and believing that what you invested in and worked so hard for the first-time to make work has been wasted and taken from you unfairly. Dreading because of a fear of the unknown and lack of motivation. Daring because of your curiosity and desire to know what it will be like the next time around. Sometimes, God has to completely tear something down in our lives so that we can begin again and do it with the right motives, the right people, in the right environment and with the right mindset. Then, there are times when God allows things and people to be taken from us unexpectedly when we have done all the right things. Job was a man devoted to God, yet he lost everything, one thing after the other from his family to his wealth. Why? God knew He could trust Job with trouble and tragedy. Through all of this, Job never cursed God, he trusted God. He embraced his struggle and fought to keep his mind and spirit in the right place to start over. The end of some things we really wanted is often the beginning of some things we really need.

Thoughts and Reflections

_____

_____

_____

_____

GOD WILL VINDICATE YOU

Devotional

#TRUSTGODFORVINDICATION

"Do not take revenge, my dear friends, but leave room for God's wrath, for it is written: "It is mine to avenge; I will repay," says the Lord."

Romans 12:19 (NIV)

Being the bigger person when you have been betrayed or done wrong can be challenging, especially when the knife came from someone you trusted or called friend. As a result, feelings of anger, resentment and hatred can surface in our hearts and the desire to retaliate to get even may cross our minds more than we would like to admit. In times like this, we must trust God to vindicate us, which means to clear of blame, defend, help and validate. We must guard our hearts, ears, eyes and lips with all diligence to not allow evil to overtake us. In some situations, when you make up your mind to do the right thing, you will be faced with opposition. You won't fit in with everybody. You will lose some friends along the way. You may spend some nights crying, tossing and turning as you fight the feelings of regret and overcome the pain of your experience. The good news is, "If God be for us, who can be against us," Romans 8:31 (NKJV)? Don't give in to the pressure to take matters and revenge into your own hands. In the words of Michelle Obama, "When they go low, we go high."

Thoughts and Reflections

_____

_____

_____

_____

_____

_____

#TRUSTGODFORVINDICATION

I AM A SURVIVOR

Devotional

#IAMASURVIVOR

"And the Lord said, 'Simon, Simon! Indeed, Satan has asked for you, that he may sift you as wheat. But I have prayed for you, that your faith should not fail; and when you have returned to Me, strengthen your brethren."

Luke 22:31-32 (NKJV)

Are you still ashamed of things from your past? Well, you survived! Are you embarrassed by things people said about your history and failures? You survived! Have you ever made bad financial and relationship decisions that you now regret? You survived! Have you ever had a near death experience? You survived that too! Do you realize how many things you have survived? There is a reason why you survived it all. Don't be deceived by the enemy's tactics to belittle your survival story. Don't allow him to cause you to focus on everything that went wrong and make you miss all the things that went right. Your survival was designed by God to become a lifeline for someone else. God has the power to take your greatest pain and give you your greatest breakthrough. Repeat these words, "I am a survivor!" What is a survivor? One who has lived to tell the story that many died in. What did not kill you made you better, wiser, and stronger.

Thoughts and Reflections

_____

_____

_____

_____

_____

_____

_____

ACKNOWLEDGEMENTS

To everyone who believed in and trusted the gifts and talents God so graciously gave me to touch and change their lives, thank you. I would like to thank my parents, Kathelyn and Sherman Dudley for carrying the gifts and talents that were passed on to me at birth, Niecy Wells for her tutelage throughout my writing process, every professor and counselor that taught me invaluable knowledge and lessons, Jeralynn Hubbard for being a beta reader and assisting with the editing process, all of my friends for their prayers and support, my Pastor, Spencer T. O'Neal and mentor, Prophetess Nicole Armstrong for pushing me to get this book out and Apostle Travis Jennings for the prophetic activation that helped me to hear the vision for this book. I will be forever grateful and appreciative for all your encouragement and support.

ABOUT THE AUTHOR

Franchetta Dudley is a practical, yet profound, prophetic emerging voice for this present generation. Academically, she received a Bachelor of Science Degree in Communication Arts from Georgia Southern University in Statesboro, Georgia and a Master of Divinity in Pastoral Care and Counseling from the Interdenominational Theological Center in Atlanta, Georgia. With over 15 years of experience in education and 20 years of experience in ministry, one of her main goals is to create and provide people with an environment wherein their lives, decision-making processes, and character can be subjectively and objectively shaped by the facts, truth, reality, and experiences advocated in the word of God. Her motto is, "When one chooses and decides to be, one becomes." She is gifted by God to encourage, motivate, challenge, and inspire individuals to be the best that they can be. Her teachings and counsel are purposed for igniting hope and speaking life into seemingly hopeless situations.

STAY CONNECTED

Thank you for reading *Helpful Hashtags*. Franchetta would like to connect with you and keep you updated on new book releases, book signings, speaking engagements, and more! Below are a few ways you can connect with the author.

FACEBOOK Franchetta Dudley Ministries
INSTAGRAM @ladyfranchettad
TWITTER @ladyfranchettad
EMAIL franchettadudleyministries@gmail.com
WEBSITE www.franchettadudley.com

www.ingramcontent.com/pod-product-compliance
Lightning Source LLC
Chambersburg PA
CBHW021227090426
42740CB00006B/417